Caterpillars Can Fly!

A Tale of Identity and Purpose

Lenore D. Greenaway

CATERPILLARS CAN FLY Copyright © 2024 Lenore D. Greenaway

All rights reserved. No part of this book may be used or reproduced in any form whatsoever without written permission, except in the case of brief quotations in critical articles or reviews.

This book is a work of fiction. Names, characters, businesses, organisations, places, events, and incidents either are the product of the author's imagination or are used fictitiously. Any resemblance to actual persons, living or dead, events, or locales is entirely coincidental.

Printed in the United Kingdom.

For more information, or to book an event, contact :
Lenore@eronelltd.com | www.LenoreLightOnline.com

Editing, illustrations, and author services by Opulent Books www.OpulentBooks.net

ISBN 978-1-916691-52-0

First Edition: 2024

Acknowledgement

All gratitude to Jesus Christ, my Lord, who called me before I was in my mother's womb. To my sisters, Jacqueline and Melrose and my nieces and nephews: Saskia, Jolaine, Kay-Jean, Jayden, Janiel, Jah-Mari, Kei-Mara and Jarrel. Thank you for your support.

Thank you to Joe Benjamin and Opulent Books for your unwavering support in assisting me to live out my purpose.

My young readers, thank you for giving me the opportunity to continue to inspire and serve you.

It was story time once again in the lush, verdant green forest, where a small monarch caterpillar named Caleb was born. The sun kissed the earth as all the animals settled themselves in comfortable positions for the usual weekly tale.

Raya the Rabbit sat in the middle of the animals that formed a circle around her as a vibrant yellow, orange and white campfire blazed and crackled, giving the much-needed light. Raya's story about the importance of change caused Caleb to reflect.

Caleb loved wiggling his way around the vast forest, exploring his surroundings and munching on leaves as he thought about all he had heard during story time. He would often daydream about all the adventures he would have, flying to new heights once he was a butterfly.

However, Caleb was also terrified of the idea of turning into a butterfly. Each time his friends would talk about the transformation process, he would shudder in palpable fear because of the unknown and the thought of losing his caterpillar identity.

One sunny day, Caleb set out on an adventure to find out more about what lay ahead for him, extremely nervous that he only had fourteen days left in his caterpillar stage.

Along his journey, he met a wise old owl named Orson who overheard Caleb's story and commented, "Dear Caleb, you are meant to transform into a butterfly. Don't be afraid, for this is your true identity and purpose. You cannot escape what must be. Go through it!"

Feeling slightly encouraged, Caleb continued his journey, but he was still petrified. By this time, fear gripped his entire being that he could think of nothing else. Soon after, he stumbled upon Sharar the snail who uttered, "Why bother going through all the trouble of transformation? Staying as a caterpillar is much easier and less scary. Stick to what you know. How can a caterpillar like you grow wings anyway? It is simply impossible! Living on the ground is perfectly fine!"

Hearing these words, Caleb felt discouraged once again, but he didn't give up. Now, news had spread throughout the forest like a wildfire about Caleb's predicament and everyone he met wanted to give him further advice.

As he continued his journey of discovery, he met a bumble bee named Zoe who shared with him all the breathtaking colours and sights of the world from a bee's-eye view. Zoe told Caleb while she buzzed away into the distance, making a figure-eight pattern, "Just imagine all of the wonderful things you'll see if you become a butterfly! You will be un…bee…lievably happy like me!"

Encouraged and uplifted again by Zoe's words, Caleb wiggled his way further into the heart of the immense forest, where ancient trees whispered secrets and dew-kissed leaves shimmered. His tiny legs clung to a vibrant green leaf as his mind was filled with thoughts of the unknown. Around him, the forest hummed with life. Ladybugs danced in their crimson tutus, bees bombilated symphonies and flapping butterflies brought a myriad of colours to the vast blue sky.

The following misty morning, as the sun peeked through emerald branches, Caleb noticed a little girl walking and picking luscious berries and wildflowers. Her eyes held the wonder and sparkle of a thousand constellations. She clutched tightly a woven brown basket which carried the contents of her foraging.

Aurea's gaze met Caleb's anxious demeanour, then she whispered with compassion in her voice, "What is the matter dear little caterpillar? You look like you are carrying the whole world on your shoulders."

Caleb explained to his new-found friend all of his worries and anxieties about going through metamorphosis – as she leant on a nearby bush and listened attentively, like nothing else mattered.

"I know you're scared, but remember, change is a part of life. Sometimes, you will feel afraid, but always face your fears so that you can become what you're meant to be.

Just like I have to learn new things constantly, you too have to embrace this change. It might seem petrifying now, but it's going to make you stronger and beautiful in a different way.

Remember, every butterfly was once a caterpillar. They too were probably scared, but look at them around us, flying high in the enormous blue sky, spreading joy and beauty wherever they go.

You have a wonderful journey ahead of you. Just believe in yourself. I wish that I could see you when you transform into a gorgeous butterfly."

Caleb's heart fluttered with hope once again. "Perhaps," he replied in a cheerful voice, "if we believe."

Moments later, Caleb then met a listless lizard who was basking in the morning sun on a rock to raise its body temperature. "Hello, my name is Caleb, what's yours?"

"I am Nechum," he responded with vigour. "Why do you look troubled?" Once again, Caleb discussed his plight with Nechum as he continued his sunbathing.

Nechum advised, "Why bother with the trouble of transformation? It is too risky anyway to agree to what you are not certain of! You don't need the hassle. Look at me. I relax all the time in my routine. What more do I need? I am comfortable crawling on the ground all the time and I am just fine and you will be too."

A chatty and friendly squirrel named Sammy was perched on a branch intently listening to their conversation, "Psst! Hey, Caleb, it's ok to be afraid little fellow. If I were you, I would not listen to Nechum's thoughtless advice. Never limit yourself in any way!"

The frightened caterpillar was not aware that there was a covenant of magnificent change that had already been spoken over his life. All he needed to do was to allow the change to take place.

"Excuse me!" interrupted a stunning butterfly which was enjoying her food from nectar rich flowers. "Your identity as a caterpillar is only a transitory stage, but rather as a beautiful butterfly, so do not be afraid. Change is a necessary part of life. Take your upgrade like me. By the way, my name is Uriel," she informed.

"Everything you need to become a butterfly is already inside of you. Your wings to take you to new heights where you have never been before are there also!" Uriel declared with exhilaration.

Uriel shared her story of transformation that was full of struggles and the end result that was worth it all.

Encouraged by Uriel's story, Caleb knew that he had to overcome his fears and embrace his sleepy transformation.

Suddenly, a flood of positive energy inundated his mind. All of the negative thoughts that he held about himself and his future were obliterated.

He then heard an unfamiliar and mysterious voice which echoed twice in his head, "Eat, grow and change. I can dream of a bigger dream than you can dream for yourself!"

Without hesitation, Caleb devoured a milkweed leaf in under five minutes. He ate and ate until he grew a spectacular two thousand seven hundred times his original weight. He was determined to live out his destiny. Now fully grown, he stopped eating.

Caleb wept with clarity as he finally realised that change was inevitable. He wiggled his way with determination on to a smooth, lined leaf, then a branch, his destiny partner, ready to begin his transformation to greatness.

He made himself comfortable, closed his eyes and sang a little rhyme out loud – about all that he learned on his adventure and the mysterious metamorphosis process which forever will be a marvel in nature.

"Expertly, I spin a chrysalis around myself…no time to linger!

My becoming chamber, where in the darkroom, (as black as a thousand midnights), I am transformed by God's finger!

Don't assume that nothing is happening because nothing can be seen!

Tremendous changes will reveal what I have never been!

Glorious beauty developed in the dark serenity,

Will manifest a brand new and unbelievable me!

No one must interfere with my struggle. When my chrysalis becomes transparent, it is my time to come out!

Ruin awaits me if this is not heeded, without a doubt!

So, I choose to be bold and all fears conquer,

My greatness, I will not delay any longer!"

Caleb gradually transformed and when he wrestled his way out, emerged from his chrysalis confinement and opened his eyes, he beheld the inconceivable. He was a totally new creature! Remarkably, he now had brightly hued brilliant orange wings with distinct black veins and snow-white spots of varied sizes, which were perfectly placed along the edges. Each of his hind wings exhibited a distinguishing black dot. He was an impressive work of art on a higher level! A wonder!

He now was an expression of what he was created to be ultimately – his new identity as a magnificent, majestic monarch butterfly.

Filled with awe, Caleb bellowed gleefully, "I am so beautiful! There was no need to be afraid. Look at me now!" His jubilant shouts jiggled their way through the statuesque trees, to every animal nearby and escaped up to the great blue sky. He felt proud of himself that he chose to be courageous to go through his transformation and accept his God-given purpose. Hidden beauty was inside him all along.

Now a unique flying insect, Caleb knew that he would not live for a long time – only a few weeks. Bubbling with excitement, he did not hesitate in flapping his wings (about twelve times per second) and took flight on his way to get energy by feeding on nectar from flowers. He exclaimed, "Yippee!!! Here I come world! I am flying high!"

He flew to new heights, exploring the world as he had never seen it before. The sights he beheld were so enthralling that he knew he had found his true purpose, bringing value to the world. This magnificent creature lived up to his name and realised that he was always brave.

He understood that greatness, power, beauty and hidden wings to soar were within him all along and that he can overcome any obstacles. And so can you.

A Message from the Author

Precious young ones, you too have greatness and beauty locked up inside of you that is waiting to be revealed. Do you want to be like Caleb the caterpillar and live out your destiny of greatness?

If yes, allow the One who created you and everything in the universe by marvellous design, to finish the work which He started in you by saying this prayer.

Dear God,

Thank You for loving me so much that You sent Your Son, Jesus Christ to die on the cross to save me. You raised Him from the dead and He is alive today. I ask Jesus to come into my heart. I confess with my mouth that Jesus Christ is Lord of my life from this day and by faith in Him, I receive eternal life. Thank You, Lord, for saving my soul. I am a child of God now and I am born again. Amen.

Monarch Butterfly Life Cycle

A butterfly develops through a process called metamorphosis. This is a Greek word that means transformation or change in shape. Butterflies have complete metamorphosis where the young is very different from the adults. Here is the full cycle below.

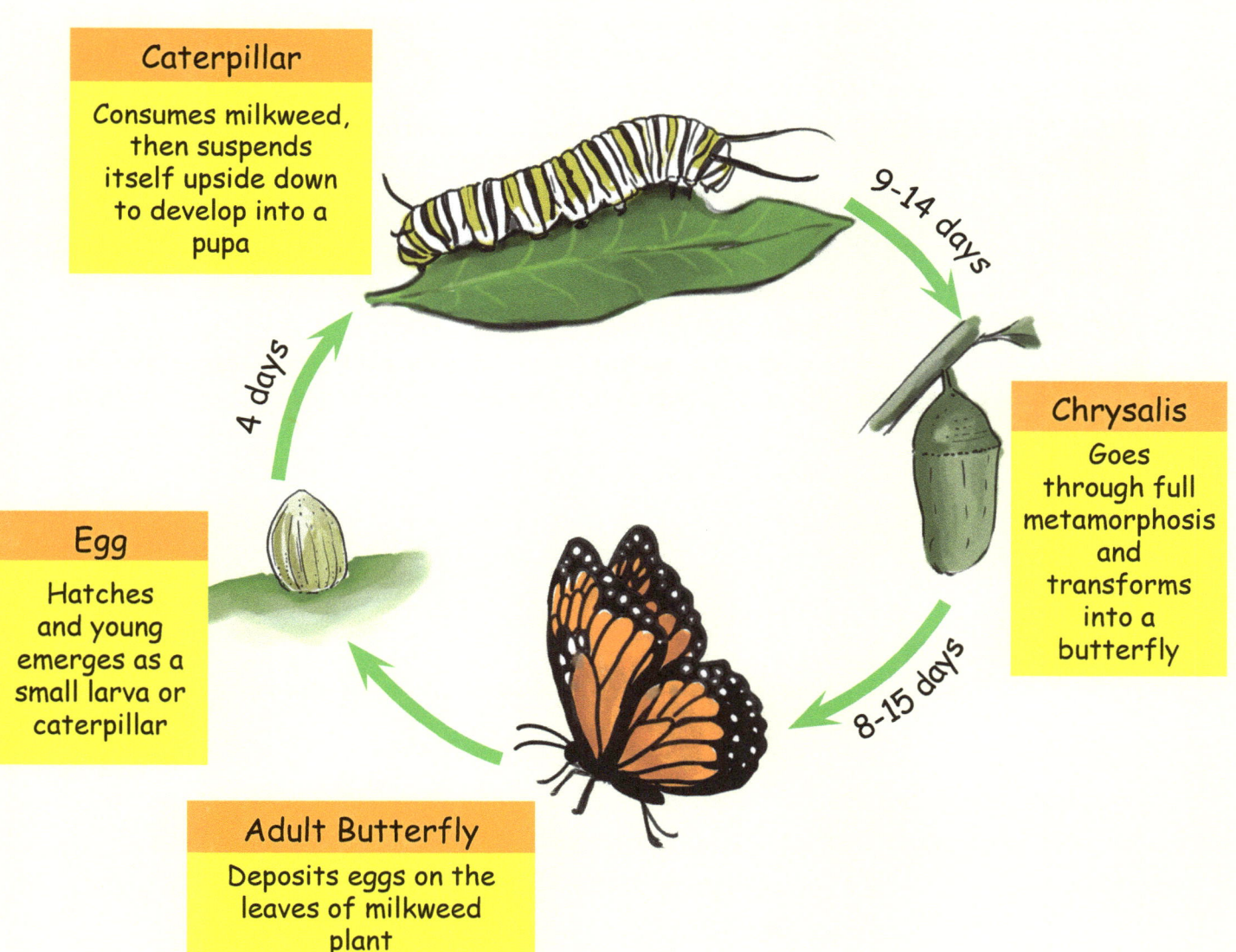

About The Author

Lenore D. Greenaway was born on the island of Montserrat in the Caribbean and resides in the United Kingdom. She holds a Bachelor of Arts Degree in Primary Education from Middlesex University. Having over three decades of teaching experience in secular education serves as a training ground, enabling her to connect with people of all ages in innovative ways. She does so with energy, passion, humour, warmth, transparency and strength to powerfully transform lives.

As an educator, author, songwriter, servant leader, Bible teacher, Reverend, entrepreneur and bridge builder, Lenore continues to make impact by devoting herself to the betterment of people through the spiritual and educational process, by God's enablement. She inspires and brings out people's passions through encouragement, motivation and helping them to envision possibilities.

She is a proponent of sustaining excellence in all aspects of her life as she makes a difference in lives, one person at a time.

For more books by Lenore D. Greenaway, please visit www.LenoreLightOnline.com. If you wish to contact the author, you can email Lenore@eronelltd.com
Phone: +44 7494 167 198

Other Children's Books by the Author

A GLITCH IN TIME….

The lives of the children in the science club and their teacher, Mrs Green, at St Francis de Sales Primary School are changed forever by the most unusual and unbelievable phenomenon.

The ordinary becomes extraordinary when their teacher is asked by Meh-EH-vehr (The Beyond) to trial their newest creation – the Virtual Reality Headset (Ra'ah Odyssey 3) and give a review.

In the process of doing this, the unimaginable happens. They are all instantaneously transported to the future – the year 2050 – and their adventure begins. Will they ever get back to the present time, or will fate be against them, condemning them to remain in the future realm forever?

www.ingramcontent.com/pod-product-compliance
Lightning Source LLC
Chambersburg PA
CBHW051321110526
44590CB00031B/4427